Great Rivers

Rivers of the World

Catherine Brereton

Raintree is an imprint of Capstone Global Library Limited, a company incorporated in England and Wales having its registered office at 264 Banbury Road, Oxford, OX2 7DY – Registered company number 6695582

www.raintree.co.uk
myorders@raintree.co.uk

Text © Capstone Global Library Limited 2018
The moral rights of the proprietor have been asserted.

Produced by Brown Bear Books Ltd:
Text: Catherine Brereton
Design Manager: Keith Davis
Editorial Director: Lindsey Lowe
Children's Publisher: Anne O'Daly
Picture Manager: Sophie Mortimer

ISBN: 978 1 4747 5401 9   ISBN: 978 1 4747 5405 7

British Library Cataloguing-in-Publication Data
A full catalogue record for this book is available from the British Library.

Acknowledgements
We would like to thank the following for permission to reproduce photographs:
Getty Images: Lloyd Cluff, 20, Eurasia Press, 19, Philip Gould, 15, Karan Su, 25, VCG, 26; iStock: Betty4249, 14, Davel5957, 13, FabioFilzi, 28 (bottom centre), Bartosz Hadyniak, 5 (bottom right), mazzzun, 11, misio69, 27, Photocech, 9, Pro-syanov, 23, Richmatts, cover, Thomas Serada, 28 (top right), USO, 21; Shutterstock: Four Oaks, 5 (top), Filipe Frazao, 7, kwest, 17, sumikophoto, 4/5; Thinkstock: Andrey Gudkov, 28 (centre left), pxhidalgo, 8

Brown Bear Books has made every attempt to contact copyright holders of material reproduced in this book. Any omissions will be rectified in subsequent printings if notice is given to the publisher. If anyone has any information please contact licensing@brownbearbooks.co.uk

Contents

Some words are shown in bold, **like this**. You can find out what they mean by looking in the glossary.

What are rivers?

Rivers are channels of fresh water flowing through the landscape. Some rivers are small. Others are huge. They carry water for hundreds of kilometres across **continents**.

The start of a river is called its **source**. The river flows from its source downhill towards the sea. The mouth of the river is where the river meets the sea. Plants and animals would not survive without fresh water from rivers. There are many important rivers around the world.

Some rivers carve deep **valleys** through the rocks.

At the mouth, rivers often spread out over a wide area. This is called an **estuary**.

Swartkops River mouth and estuary, South Africa

Colorado River, Grand Canyon, Arizona, USA

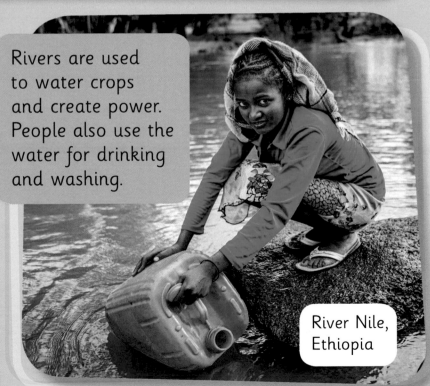

Rivers are used to water crops and create power. People also use the water for drinking and washing.

River Nile, Ethiopia

The Amazon

The Amazon is a huge river. It carries a fifth of all the world's river water. The river starts as lots of small **streams** high in the Andes Mountains and flows to the Atlantic Ocean.

The Amazon is the world's second longest river.

Where: South America

How long: 6,400 km (4,000 miles)

Countries it flows through: Peru, Colombia, Brazil

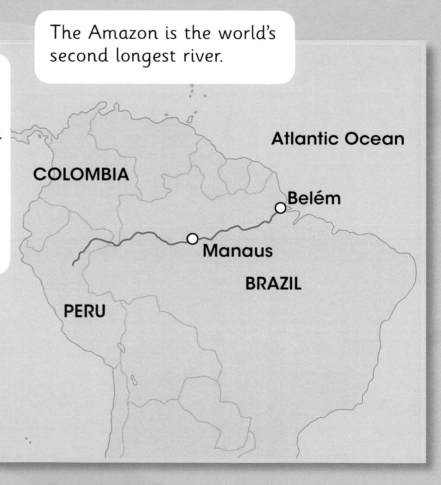

Atlantic Ocean

COLOMBIA

Belém

Manaus

BRAZIL

PERU

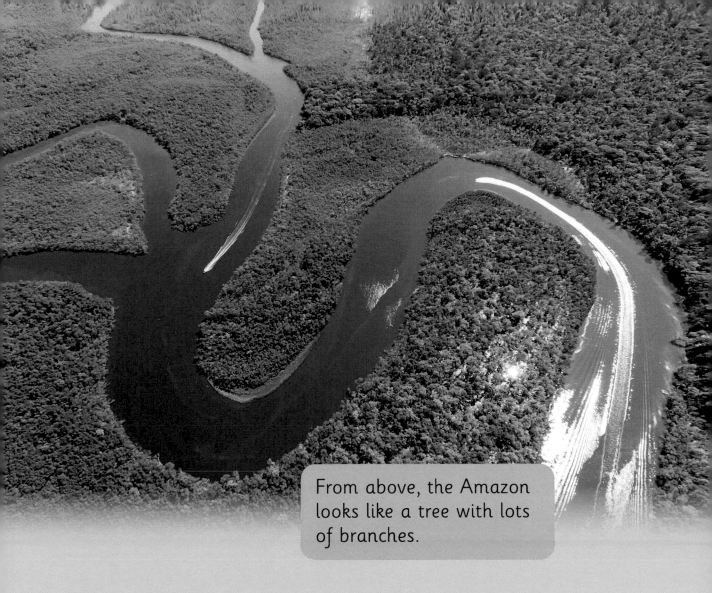

From above, the Amazon looks like a tree with lots of branches.

Smaller rivers join the main river as it travels along. These are called **tributaries**. The Amazon has around 1,100 tributaries. Together they cover an area called the Amazon **basin**. The basin covers roughly 40 per cent of the South American **continent**.

The world's largest **rainforest** covers the Amazon basin. This great rainforest is important for the **climate** of the whole planet. But people are cutting down the trees for timber. They also want to use the land for **mining** and farming.

Over 40,000 different types of plants can be found in the Amazon rainforest.

Jaguars are the largest South American big cat. They live in the Amazon river **basin**.

The Amazon rainforest is home to an amazing number of animals. There are around 1,300 bird species and 430 mammal species. There are also alligators, snakes, and around 3,000 species of freshwater fish in the Amazon River.

The Ganges

The Ganges starts in the Himalayan mountains. It flows through India and Bangladesh. Then it joins with the River Brahmaputra to make one of the biggest **deltas** in the world.

More than 400 million people live in the Ganges river **basin**.

Where: South Asia

How long: 2,510 km (1,560 miles)

Countries it flows through: India, Bangladesh

NEPAL

Kanpur
Allahabad
Varanasi
Patna

INDIA

BANGLADESH

Bay of Bengal

People bathe in the Ganges at the city of Varanasi, India.

The Ganges is a special river for **Hindus**. They believe it is **holy** to bathe in the water. Many people gather to do this at festivals along the Ganges. One important festival is Diwali, the festival of light. People celebrate with lights and fireworks.

The Mississippi

The Mississippi River starts at Lake Itasca and flows southwards through the centre of the United States to the Gulf of Mexico. This mighty river is one of the busiest waterways in the world.

The name Mississippi is a native American name meaning 'big river'.

Where: North America

How long: 3,766 km (2,340 miles)

Countries it flows through: The United States

CANADA

Minneapolis St. Paul

USA

St. Louis

Memphis

New Orleans

Gulf of Mexico

The city of St. Paul on the Mississippi has 26 miles (41 km) of riverfront.

Towns and cities are often built on river banks. The Mississippi has been a major transport route since the 1800s. Then, huge **steamboats** carried passengers and goods along the river. Today, **barges** carry millions of tonnes of goods on the Mississippi, including grain, cotton and coal.

The Mississippi is very important for wildlife. More than 350 fish species, more than 300 bird species and around 50 mammal species live in or beside the river. There are also alligators, turtles and many different frogs and toads.

Alligators lie in the sun on the banks of the Mississippi.

The Mississippi River meets the sea at the delta, just south of the city of New Orleans.

As the Mississippi nears the sea, the water flow slows down. The river becomes a wide, flat area with sandbanks and islands. This is called a **delta**. The Mississippi delta is a low-lying, swampy marshland. **Dams** and **levees** help to protect towns and cities from floods.

The Murray

The Murray River flows from high up in the Snowy Mountains, through south-east Australia, to the Indian Ocean. Along with its main **tributary**, the River Darling, it forms the huge Murray-Darling river **basin**.

Where: South-east Australia

How long: 2,530 km (1,570 miles)

Countries it flows through: Australia

The Murray flows through some of the driest areas in Australia.

AUSTRALIA

Waikerie

Mildura

Murray Bridge

Wodonga

Indian Ocean
(also called the Southern Ocean)

The Murray River provides millions of homes in Australia with water supplies.

The Murray River flows through a dry landscape. Its water allows crops to grow and wildlife to survive. People use the water in their homes. The river needs to be looked after and kept clean so that there will be enough water in the future.

The Nile

The Nile has been important to people for thousands of years. It provides water for a huge area of Africa and is the longest river in the world.

The Nile is made up of the White Nile and the Blue Nile.

Where: North-east Africa

How long: 6,695 km (4,160 miles)

Countries it flows through: Uganda, South Sudan, Sudan, Ethiopia, Egypt

Mediterranean Sea

Cairo

EGYPT — Luxor

Khartoum

SUDAN

Juba ETHIOPIA

SOUTH SUDAN

UGANDA Kampala

Lake Victoria

The ancient Egyptians travelled up and down the Nile in boats like these.

The ancient Egyptians built their **civilisation** along the Nile. The river flooded every summer. The floods left behind thick black mud that made the soil very good for growing crops.

The Aswan High Dam is a huge **dam** on the River Nile. It has a power station. It uses the energy of water to work machines called **generators**, which produce electricity. They create more than half of Egypt's total power.

The Aswan High Dam took ten years to build. It was finished in 1970.

Hippos spend most of the day in the water to keep cool.

Hundreds of different animals live near the Nile. Once, hippopotamuses lived all along the Nile. Now they are only found in a swampy part of the river in South Sudan. Some hippos live in other rivers in Africa, too.

The Volga

The Volga is the longest river in Europe.
It begins as a small **stream** in the Valdai Hills,
then flows slowly to its mouth at the Caspian Sea.
Long stretches of the river freeze solid every winter.

The Volga river **valley** is an important wheat-growing area. It is also rich in minerals.

Where: European Russia

How long: 3,530 km (2,190 miles)

Countries it flows through: Russia

RUSSIA

Yaroslavl

Novgorod

Kazan

Simbirsk

Volgograd

Astrakhan

Caspian Sea

Some sturgeon can grow up to 3 metres (10 feet) in length!

The Volga is home to huge sturgeon fish. These are valuable to fishermen because the eggs of the sturgeon, called caviar, are an expensive food. However, the sturgeon is **endangered** because of too much fishing and **pollution** in the river.

The Yangtze

The Yangtze starts on the high Plateau of Tibet. It runs for miles through mountains, then flows into the East China Sea. It is the longest river in Asia. Before 1950 there were no bridges across the river. Now there are hundreds!

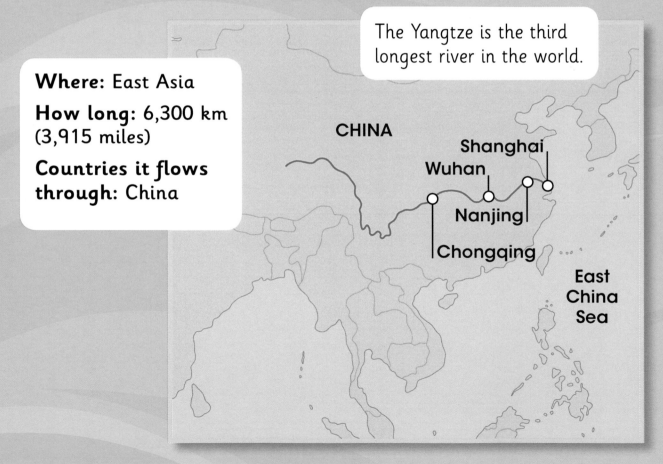

The Yangtze is the third longest river in the world.

Where: East Asia

How long: 6,300 km (3,915 miles)

Countries it flows through: China

CHINA

Shanghai
Wuhan

Nanjing

Chongqing

East China Sea

Rice grows well in fields called terraces. They are kept flooded by the river water.

Rivers are important for farming in China. The river water helps crops to grow. The Yangtze river **basin** is a big grain-growing area. Farmers grow rice, wheat and barley.

The Three Gorges **Dam** on the Yangtze is one of the biggest dams in the world. It produces electricity but also causes problems. More than a million people lost their homes when the land was flooded to make the dam. The dam also destroyed wildlife.

The Three Gorges Dam produces about a tenth of China's electricity supply.

Despite the beauty of the scenery in the Three Gorges valley, the water of the Yangtze is badly polluted.

As well as the dam, the Three Gorges **valley** is famous for its beautiful scenery. Many people take tourist boats to explore the valley. However, the river is badly **polluted**. Factories, farms and townspeople spill harmful chemicals into the water. This kills fish and is dangerous for people.

Other world rivers

The River Rhine is a major European transport route. Over 20 medieval castles and palaces can be seen along the river between Bingen and Koblenz.

The River Danube flows through ten European countries and four capital cities including Vienna, Austria. A cycle trail covers the entire river length!

The Congo is a giant river in Africa. It flows through huge areas of **rainforest**. Animals living there include the rare bonobo ape.

The Rio Grande forms the border between Mexico and Texas, in the United States. Scientists worry that long stretches of the river are drying up.

The highest **waterfall** in the world is Angel Falls in Venezuela. Here the waters of the Churun River fall an incredible 979 metres (3,212 feet).

The world's first **civilisations** appeared in Mesopotamia. This was the land between the Tigris and Euphrates rivers in the Middle East.

Location of rivers

1. Mississippi
2. Rio Grande
3. Churun
4. Amazon
5. Rhine
6. Danube
7. Tigris and Euphrates
8. Nile
9. Congo
10. Volga
11. Ganges
12. Yangtze
13. Murray

Glossary

barge long, flat boat that can carry heavy loads

basin the area of land drained by a river and all its tributaries

civilisation particular society at a particular time and place

climate the average weather pattern in a place over many years

continent one of seven huge areas of land on Earth

dam huge, strong wall that holds back the flow of a river

delta flat area at the mouth of a river where the river drops sediment

endangered in danger of dying out

estuary the mouth of a large river where it meets the sea

generator machine that produces electricity

Hindu person who follows the religion called Hinduism

holy special to the people of a particular religion

levee raised bank built along the side of a river to stop it overflowing

mining digging minerals, such as coal, metals or gold, out of the ground

pollution anything that is harmful or poisonous to the environment

rainforest forest where it is wet and rainy all year round

source where something begins

steamboat type of boat that has a steam-powered engine

stream small, narrow river that often feeds into a larger river

tributary smaller river or stream that flows into a bigger river

valley area of low ground between hills or mountains

waterfall place where a river rushes over a steep drop

Find out more

Books

A River, Marc Martin (Templar, 2016)

Rivers (Our Earth in Action), Chris Oxlade (Wayland, 2014)

Rivers (Where on Earth), Susie Brooks (Wayland, 2015)

Websites

www.bbc.co.uk/education/clips/zjxsb9q
Read Lissl's story of life in the Three Gorges area of China.

www.enchantedlearning.com/geography/rivers/majorrivers.shtml
This website has maps, facts and figures about hundreds of rivers.

www.abc.net.au/btn/topic/riverkids.htm
Watch a goup of children talking about life along the Murray River.

Places to visit

If you are travelling, here are some places you might enjoy:

Murray River Trail
www.murrayriver.com.au/kayaking-canoeing/murray-bridge-canoe-trail/
Paddle up the Murray River and discover the rich history of Murray Bridge. Drop in at the visitor centre for other highlights in the area.

Mississippi National River and Recreation Area
www.nps.gov/miss/index.htm
Extensive river park with visitor centres highlighting the history and science of the Mississippi River.

Aswan Travel Guide
www.world-guides.com/africa/egypt/aswan/
Visit the city of Aswan, the Aswan Dam and the Abu Simbel World Heritage site on the Nile.

Index